Color By Number for Kids

Color By Number 1St Grade

MDK Publications

Copyright 2015 Marshall Kids

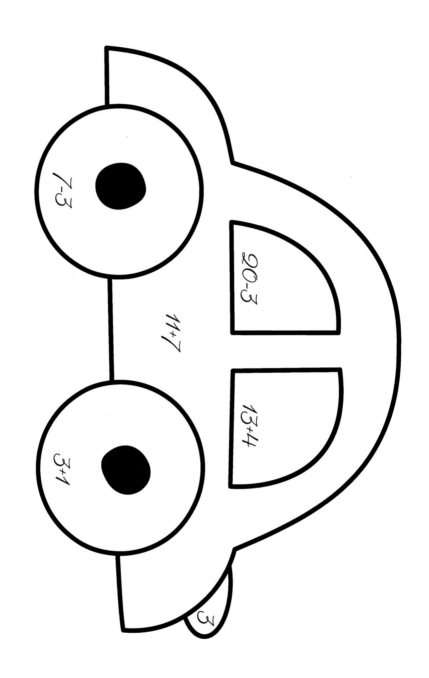

7-3

20-3

11+7

13+4

3+1

3

18

17

4

3

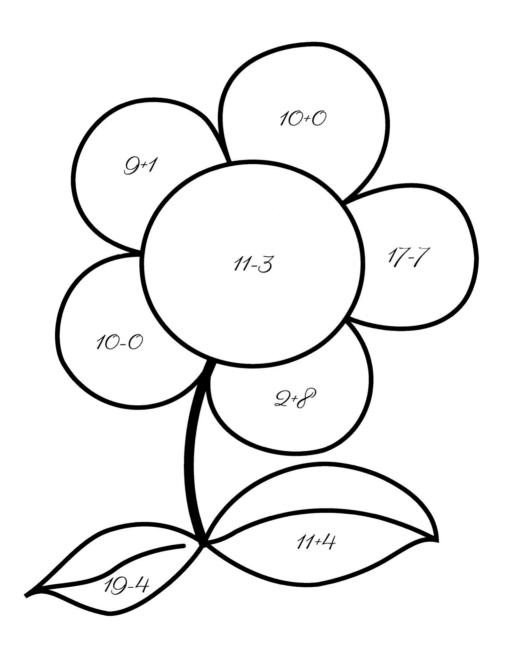

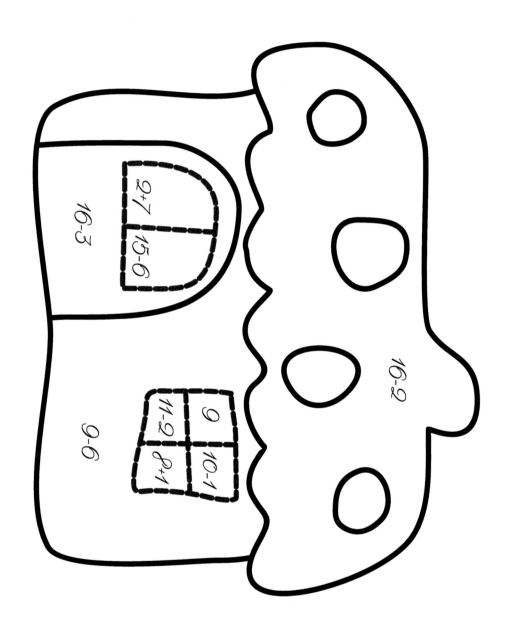

14

13

6

3

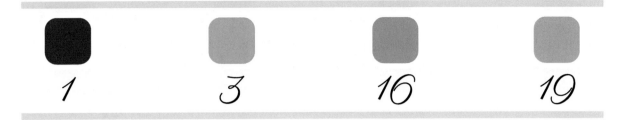

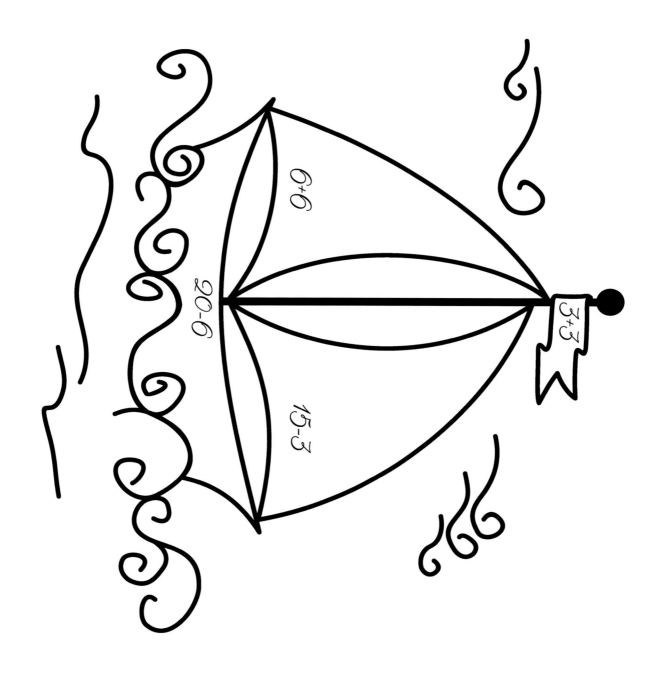

14

12

6

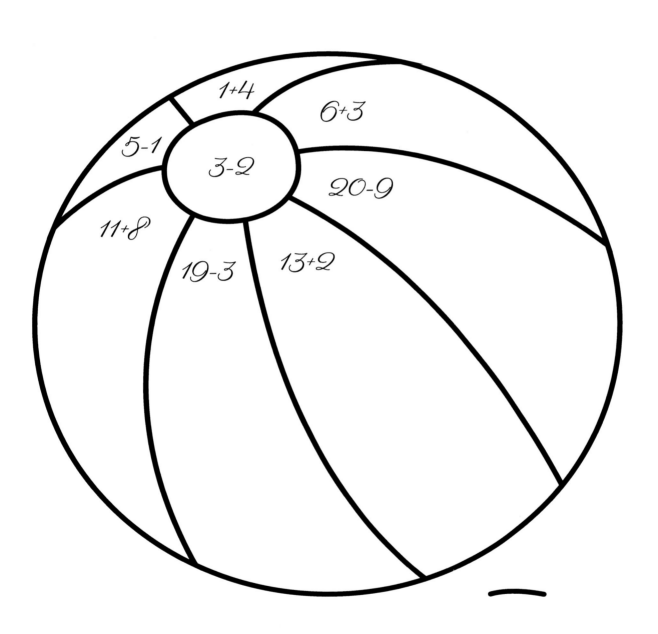

1   2   12   17   19

| 1 | 3 | 11 | 13 |

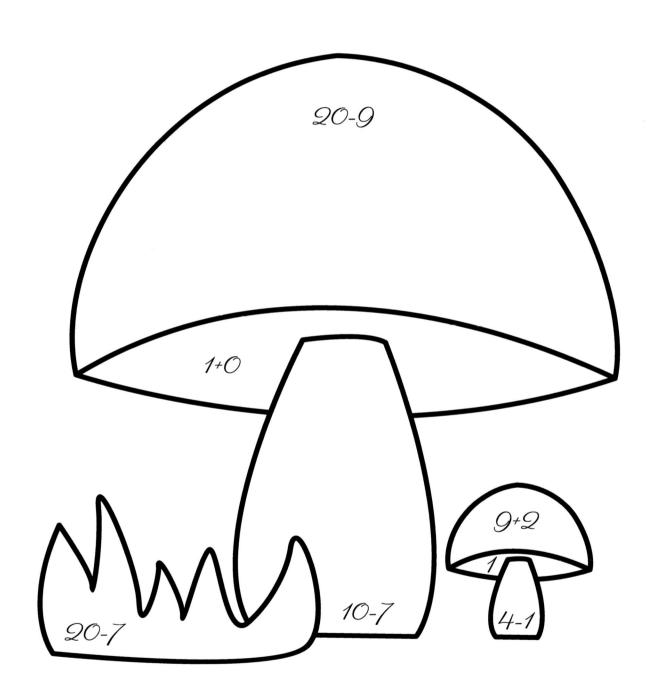

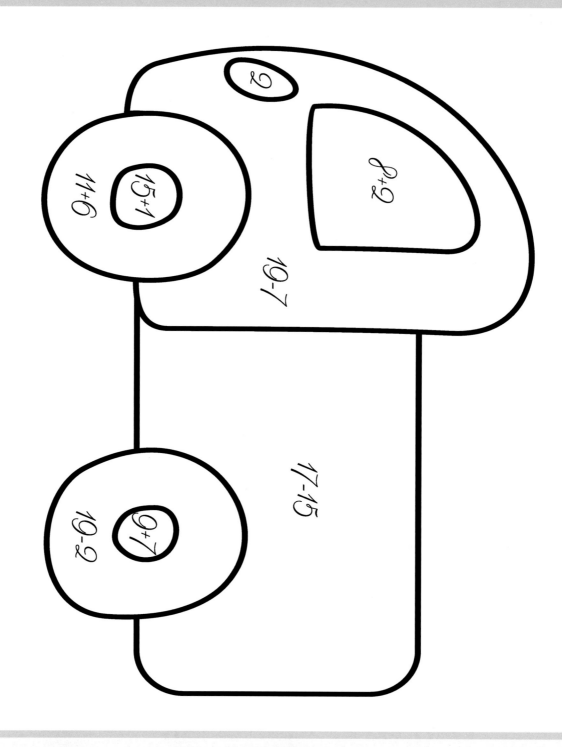

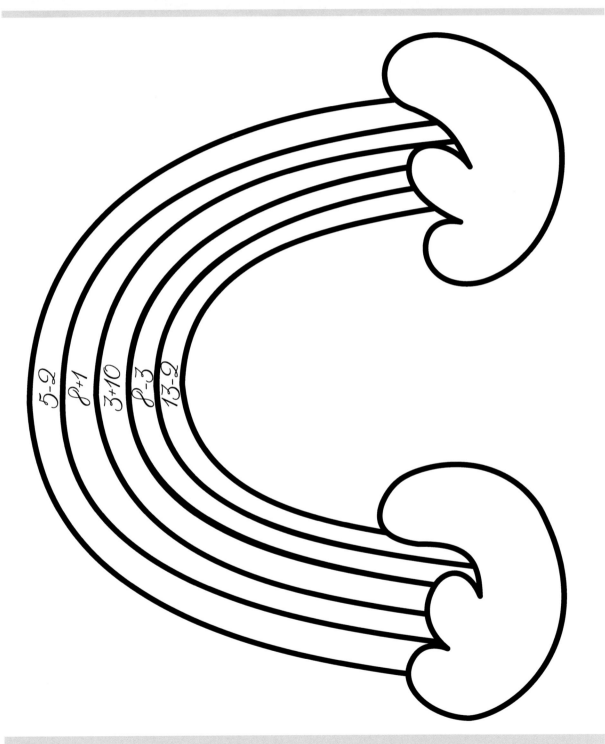

5   9   15   16

COLOR by NUMBERS

Use the color guide below to color the toy town buildings.
Color the grass green and the trees dark green. Color the sky light blue and
the sun yellow. Color other things and beings as you want!

GUIDE:

1 - Red
2 - Orange
3 - Yellow
4 - Green
5 - Dark Green

6 - Light Blue
7 - Blue
8 - Purple

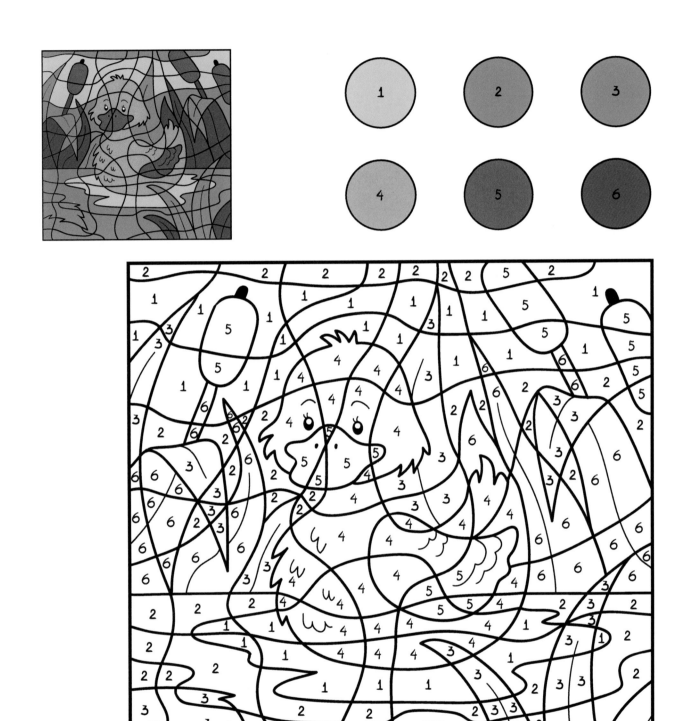

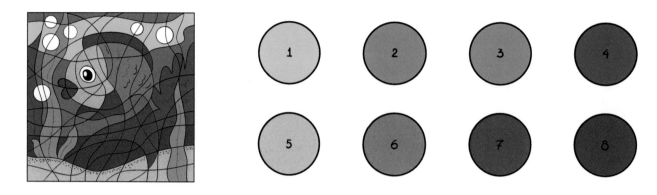

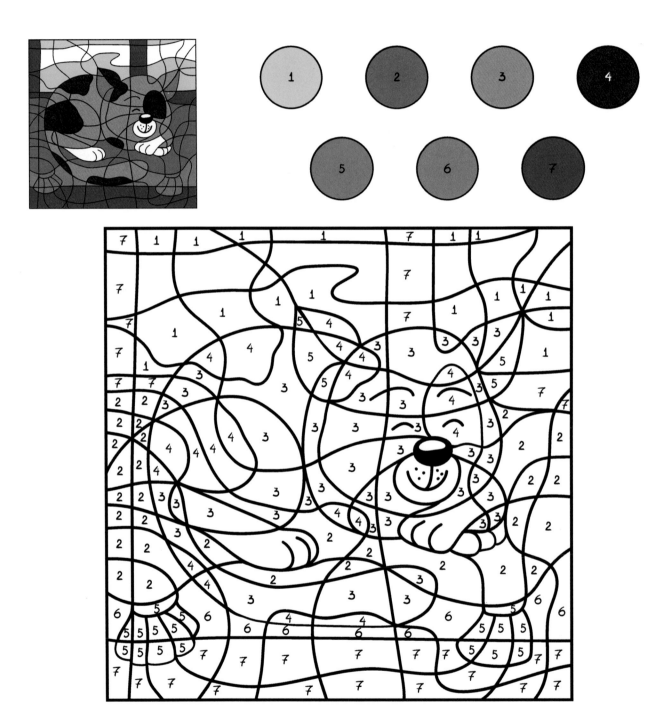

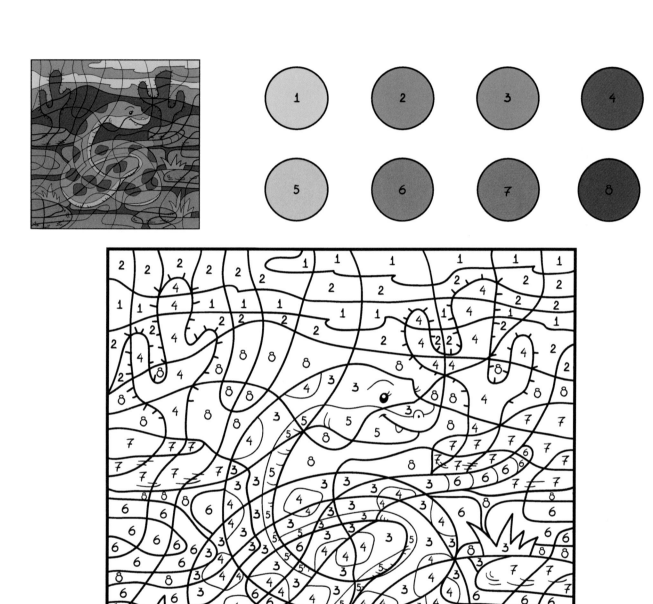

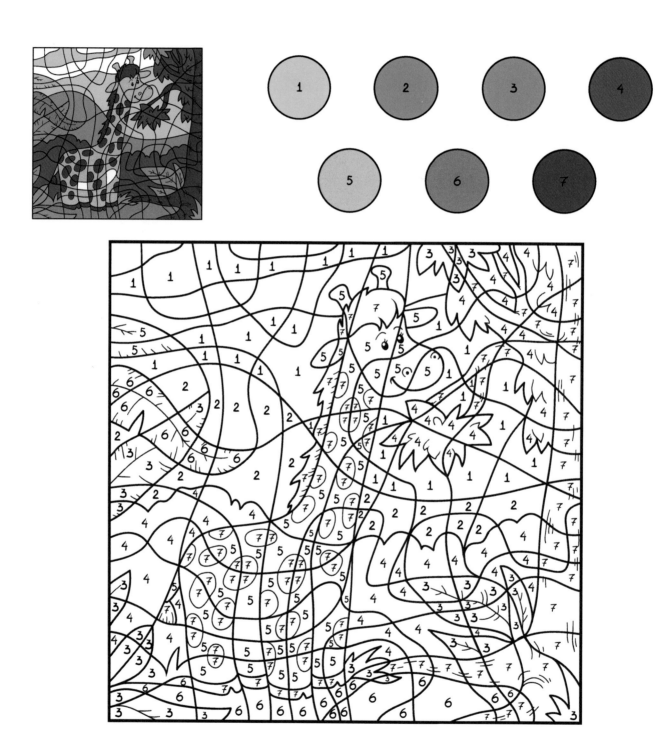

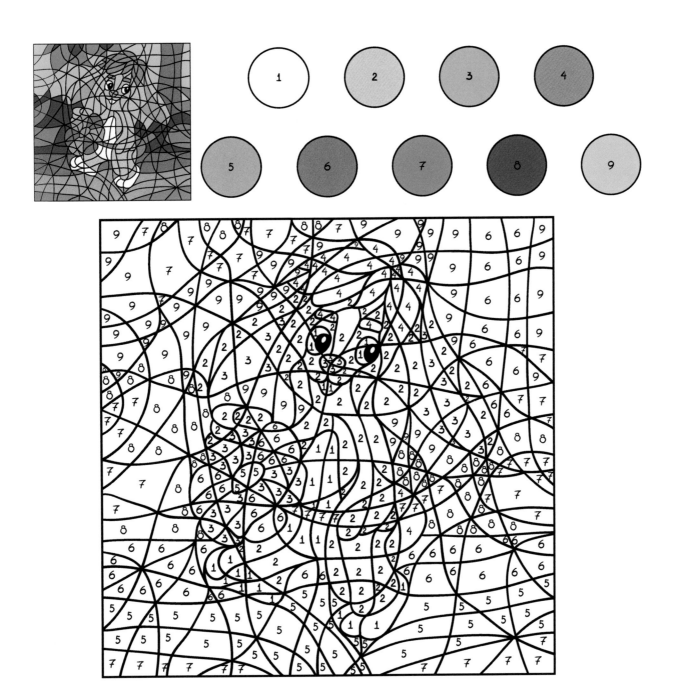

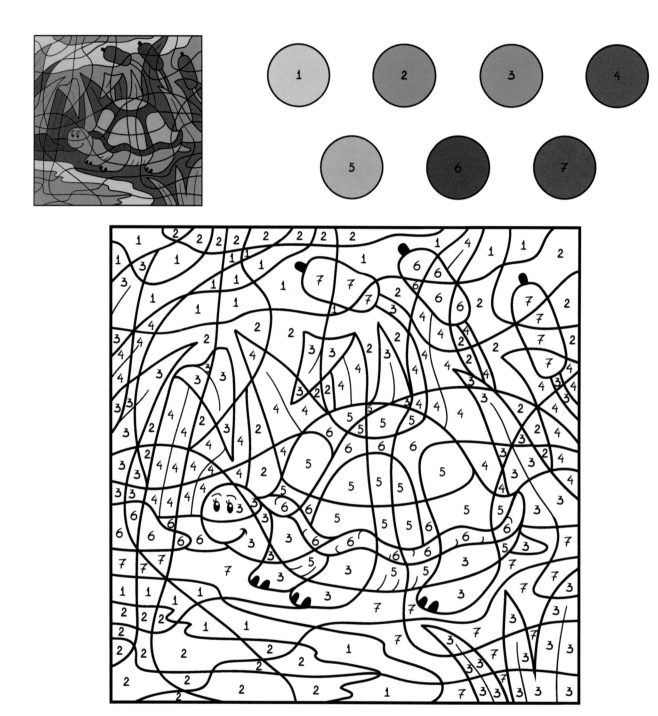

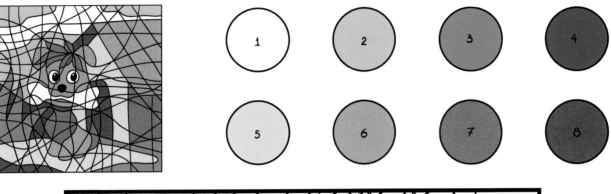

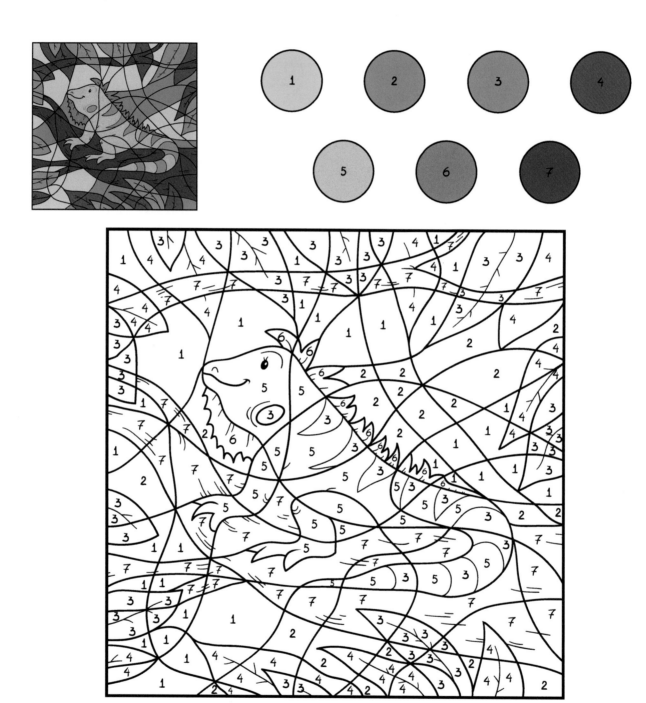

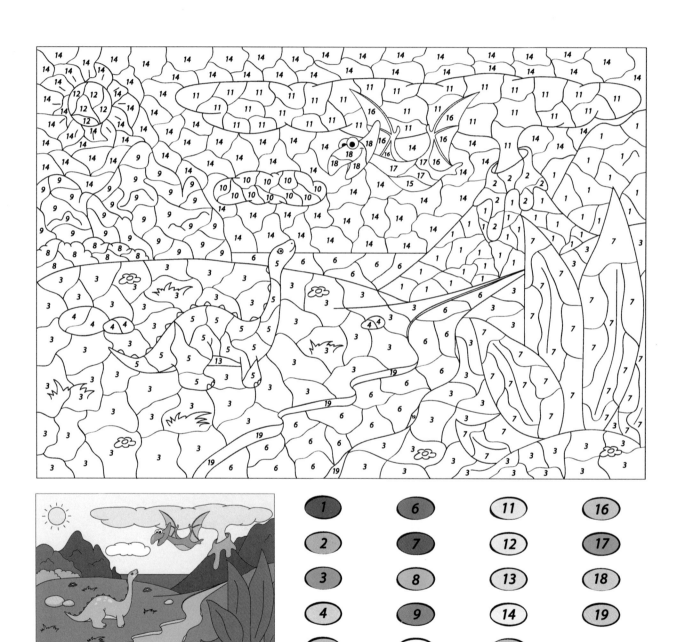

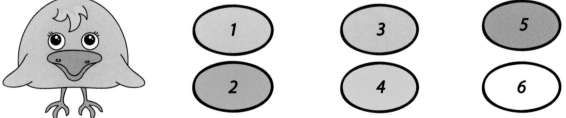

2+1 =

4-2 =

1+3 =

5-4 =

1+4 =

3+3 =

3+4 =

10-2 =

Made in the USA
Middletown, DE
01 April 2019